Volcano Blast

Haydn Middleton • **Jon Stuart**

Contents

OXFORD
UNIVERSITY PRESS

Macro Marvel
(billionaire inventor)

Welcome to Micro World!

Macro Marvel invented Micro World – a micro-sized theme park where you have to shrink to get in.

A computer called **CODE** controls Micro World and all the robots inside – MITEs and BITEs.

A MITE

A BITE

Disaster strikes!

CODE goes wrong on opening day.
CODE wants to shrink the world.

Macro Marvel is trapped inside the park ...

Enter Team X!

Four micro agents – *Max, Cat, Ant* and *Tiger* – are sent to rescue Macro Marvel and defeat CODE.

Mini Marvel joins Team X.

Mini Marvel
(Macro's daughter)

In the last book ...

* Rex was scared by the BITE's roar and ran away.

* He fell into a crack in the earth and Max, Tiger and Mini fell in too!

* Tiger dug them out in the Driller.

**CODE key
(9 collected)**

You are in the
Forbidden Valley zone.

3

Before you read

Sound checker
Say the sound.

re   **our**

Sound spotter
Blend the sounds.

c	o	l	our

c	e	n	t	re

c	oo	l	er

Into the zone
Do you know any facts about volcanoes?

4

Volcano Facts

Ant liked finding out about nature. "I'm reading about the behaviour of volcanoes," he told Cat.

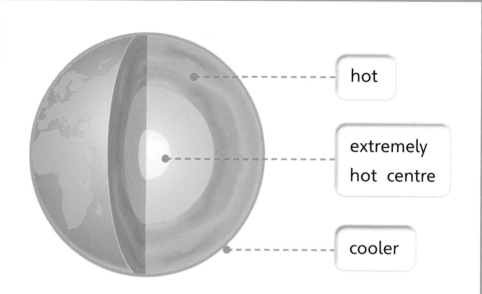

hot

extremely hot centre

cooler

The centre of our planet is much hotter than the ground we walk on. Not far below our feet it can get really hot too.

lava

Some underground rocks get so hot, they melt and boil! This boiling rock is called lava. The colour of most hot lava is red.

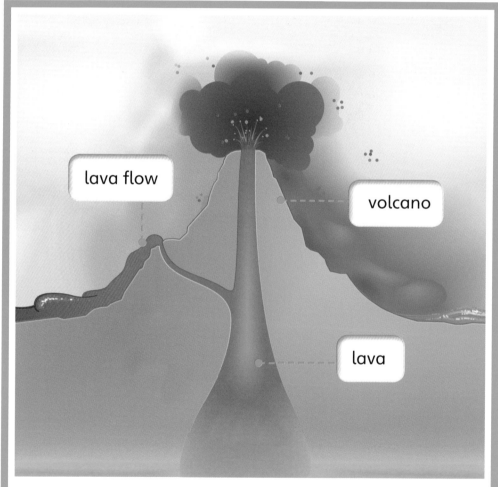

lava flow

volcano

lava

Sometimes, the red-hot lava has so much force it has to shoot out of the ground. That is when volcanoes erupt.

This lava is boiling hot!

ash cloud

When volcanoes erupt, lots of ash gets into the air. This can block the sunlight.

Some volcanoes don't erupt for a long time. People live near them because the soil is good for growing crops.

"Volcanoes are really hot and really cool!" said Ant. "Let's take a look."

Now you have read ...
Volcano Facts

Take a closer look
What would you find on a story page and an information page? Decide where each label should go.

Story page	Information page

diagrams with labels

pictures of characters

photos

characters' speech

facts

Thinking time
Ant said that volcanoes are "really hot and really cool!" What do you think he meant?

I want a closer look at this volcano!

Before you read

Sound checker

The sound to remember when you are reading this book.

re   our

Word alert

Blend the sounds. Listen for the /uh/ sound in these words.

fire   entire

vapour   humour

Into the zone

Can you remember who has just walked along the path to the volcano?

Set in Stone

Chapter 1 – Monster in the Mist

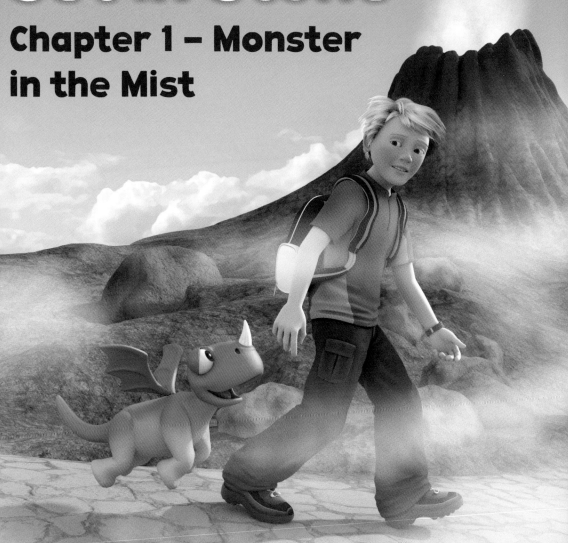

Tiger and Rex had found the volcano too. They walked up the path.

The air was hot and vapour hung all around. It was hard to see and it felt very eerie. Tiger saw a big shape through the mist.

"Look out, Rex!" he called. "I can see some sort of creature. It could be a vulture – or a dinosaur!"

Just then, the vapour cleared a little. "Phew!" said Tiger. "It's just a signpost!"

Volcano View

Earthquake Experience

Then they heard a rumbling noise ...

Chapter 2 – New Danger

At last Cat and Ant reached the platform at Volcano View.

Suddenly, the BITE pressed the controls.

"Quick! Get off the volcano! It's erupting!" yelled Ant.

Cat and Ant ran fast and managed to make their way down the volcano.

"Phew, we're safe now," said Ant.
"Not yet," replied Cat. "Look behind you!"
Hot lava was only a few metres away!

The entire volcano shook. Cat and Ant fell down and stared as the river of lava sloshed around them! They yelled in terror.

Tiger and Rex heard the screams. "That sounds like Cat and Ant!" said Tiger. "Quick, Rex, take a look."

Chapter 3 – A Favour For Friends

Cat and Ant noticed something. The lava was cold, not hot. It was fake!

They just had time to smile at each other before they had a new shock. The fake lava turned rock hard straight away. They were trapped!

Cat and Ant could see no way to escape.

"I hope the BITE doesn't find us trapped here!" said Ant.
"Look!" shouted Cat.

Rex came flying towards them.
"Snorp, snorp!" he laughed when he saw his two friends.
"This is no time for humour, Rex," cried Cat. "Help us!"

Rex blasted fire at the hard lava. At once it melted, setting Cat and Ant free. "Thank you, Rex," said Ant. "I wanted to get close to the volcano but this was *too* close!"

Now you have read ...
Set in Stone

Thinking time
Why did Cat and Ant yell in terror when the lava sloshed around them?

Take a closer look
Choose the correct word to complete the sentences.

liquid	solid

When the lava exploded from the volcano it was _____ .

It turned _____ and trapped Cat and Ant.

When Rex blasted fire at the lava, it became _____ again.

I'm going to stop Team X and Mini!